Giovanni Di Capua

TARQUINIA

translated by Elisa Pierandrei and Maria Scipioni

SCIPIONI

1

D0068613

SCIPIONI - March 2007
01018 Valentano (VT) Loc. Valle dell'Aia
Tel.: 0761 420198 Fax 0761 453686
Web site: www.leggendogodendo.com e-mail:fescipi@tin.it
Printed by: Industria Grafica La Cassandra - Pineto (TE)

TWO CITIES

Tarquinia, the ancient Etruscan lucumonia, before being defeated by the Roman Empire (*Tarch[u]na* in Etruscan, *Tarquinii* in Latin), was one of the most powerful cities in Etruria. It was stood on the calcareous hill of the fortified Civita, naturally bordered on three sides by steep cliffs and rivers called Saint Savino and Albucci, tributaries of the river Marta, which comes from Lake Bolsena.

Tarquinia is located on the Tyrrhenian coast, about 100 km from Rome, and 6 km from the sea. Thanks to many historical records, we know that this area has been populated since the Copper and Bronze Ages and grew in importance with a further development of human settlements towards the end of the Bronze Age (12th-10th century B.C.).

During the Iron Age the number of former villages gradually decreased. It seems there was a tendency to gather together among the population in a single area, close to fields and natural route of communication. However, during the 9th-8th century B.C., apart from the Civita, there were large villages built in Monterozzi area (we do not know if they were under the control of the main one), on the evidence of settlements discovered in the so called necropolis. There, the most important funeral monuments of the historic city of Tarquinia are concentrated.

The paintings of its frescoed tombs represent a unique heritage for the knowledge of Etruscans. A genuine art-gallery, which throws light upon the customs, the life and the death of a population still surrounded by mystery. The Etruscan civilisation, as that Egyptian, holds a peculiar fascination for some people to this day.

The tomb decorations inspired by daily life, banquets, indoors and outdoor games, show the Etruscans philosophy of life and their religious belief, which also influenced the Roman cult, e.g. the omens made by the Augurs.

The modern city of Tarquinia is 3 km away from the ancient

Etruscan city and it partly covers the territory which expanded rapidly from the 5th century A.D., around a new built-up area known as Corneto.

The process of modifying the urban social groups of people were influenced and stimulated by coming into frequent contact with the Greek World, during the eighth century B.C.. Especially, it took to increasing the urbanisation. Greeks, in the first place through their western colonies, seem to have deeply influenced this stock: acquisition of new technologies, intensification of metal and pottery trades. New factories in imitation of these objects were set up, by means of Greek immigrants and then by Etruscans.

Meanwhile, Tarquinia probably kept under control the mines of the mountains of Tolfa: there is still evidence of a period of great prosperity, shown by the tombs and in urban traces. Towards the end of the eighth century B.C., a new culture, having a Greek-oriental turn of thought, arose at the end of the urbanisation process and from the development of a real aristocratic cast with its impressive burial monuments and tomb furnishings. The Civita became the only settlement of some importance, and the social stratification became more prominent. In this connection, near huts and the graves of poorer citizens, there have been found traces of new dwellings made of stone, and different kinds of burial mounds.

During the seventh century B.C. Tarquinia, according to ancient sources, was still described as a powerful and prosperous centre, but it was losing wealth and power compared to the neighbouring cities. Probably, Cerveteri succeeded in keeping under control the mountains of Tolfa. At the end of this century, Tarquinia and Veio were isolated in the southern coastal area of Etruria.

During the end of the seventh century and the beginning of the sixth B.C., Tarquinia recovered its old prosperity again, when, under the influence of the town of Vulci, Etruscan-Corinthian pottery workshops were functioning, producing objects of excellent artistic quality. Objects made in Tarquinia were exported as far as Carthage.

The construction of the Gravisca port is not unconnected with this revival period. In its surroundings was constructed an important emporium too, frequented by merchants and foreign craftsmen.

The area of Tarquinia, not much explored at that time, was not yet known in its full width. Perhaps later it expanded to Plain of the Queen where, since the first half of the sixth century B.C., a magnificent sanctuary was built. Two centuries later there was built the magnificent temple of the **Altar of the Queen**.

The city which, at the end of the sixth century, extended its power into the hinterland as far as the Lake Bolsena, after the second quarter of the fifth century suffered from the political and social crisis due to external causes, financial straits of the aristocracy and class tensions.

In Cere and Veio there prevailed democratic or radical or tyrranical solutions, but in Tarquinia oligarchy became more solid and strong, and several privileged families developed and began to emerge. However, difficulties in these years imposed restrictions on the economic power of both lower classes and old aristocracy. A reduction of Attic pottery imports, a stagnation of building trade and handicrafts were the results. The Gravisca port and its sanctuary suffered badly.

A revival period (fourth century B.C.) followed the political, economical and cultural crisis of the fifth century B.C., and Tarquinia overcame Cere and other Etruscan cities in wealth. In this period, Tarquinia, not concerned by Celtic invasions (about 385 B.C.), finally colonised the territories conquered before. This new, flourishing state allowed a rapid recovery of all activities.

Impressive burial monuments decorated by paintings, with sarcophagi and funerary sculptures in stone, reflect the eminent social position of new aristocratic classes, but several inscriptions on walls and sarcophagi show as the gradual process of making the government increasingly democratic was developed.

However, during the fourth century B.C., when Tarquinias expansion was at its peak, a bitter struggle with Rome took place and, after a forty years truce, in 311 B.C., the Etruscans had to confront the Romans again. After the last in vain attempt of the Etruscan cities to oppose Rome, the Romans conquered the whole territory. In 204 B.C. Tarquinia allied with Rome in struggles against the Carthaginians.

In 181 B.C. the Roman colony of Gravisca was founded on the coast. After 90 B.C. Tarquinia obtained the right of Roman citizenship and became a municipality. It gained a little prestige during the Antonini dynasty, that is to say Antonino Pio, Marco Aurelio, Lucio Vero, Commodo, Settimio Severo, Caracalla.

Decadence was inexorable in the late Imperial period and the barbarian invasions of Italy (specially the Visigothic one of King Alarigo in 408) marked its ruin. In the seventh-eight century the Civita was abandoned, but it took importance again in the Middle Ages when it was rebuilt on the next hill where the present town stands. The town, at that time known as Corneto, developed as a rich commercial and agrarian centre. In the middle of the eleventh century it was a feudal estate of the Countess *Matilde di Canossa.*

It is well documented that towards the fourteenth century, Tarquinia and Corneto co-existed, although the latter one was more important. To the former **castrum** (a Latin word for hamlet or fortified towns) was added the Castle construction.

During the ninth and tenth centuries a solid, defensive surrounding walls were built. Some remains of these boundary walls still survive.

In the thirteenth century Corneto developed as a free commune. In 1245, it withstood a siege by Frederick the Second but the town surrendered in 1355 to the Albornoz and Orsini families, after a long struggle. In the sixteenth century it fell into the hands of the Church, after an interval during which it was under the Vitelleschi family control.

The town planning of the twelfth and thirteenth centuries divided Corneto into terziere (quarters): the directrix of the Road of Towers divided the town into two sectors, the Hill Terziera (as far as S. James, the Saviour and the Our Lady of Annunciation areas) and the Valley Terziera, which included the lower area of fortified walls. Castro Novo Terziera included the right side of the city, delimited by the climb going from the Vitelleschi palace to the Belvedere of Alberata. The Castle area was excluded from the urban periphery. The port of Gravisca, a vital point between Pisa and Terracina, known as Clementino Port, was reorganised and increased in wealth by the works undertaken by Pope Clemente XII. In that way, Corneto stipulated a commercial treaty with Pisa, Genoa and Venice, and it became a good place where people and goods could be landed. For example, in 1190 it provided a convenient landing for the navy of Richard the Lion-Hearth and in 1217 for other crusaders.

Between the twelfth and the thirteenth centuries the fashion for towers, symbols of political and economical power became marked. The most important families built towers that were standing either alone or were part of other buildings. The higher the tower, the more important was the family.

Just about twenty of the former towers still rise above the roofs downtown in the city. The majority of them were destroyed or cut off during the struggles of the commune.

The high towers and the city-walls show a certain similarity to Corneto and San Gimignano, in Tuscany.

In 1922 the city regained its former name of Tarquinia.

Tomb of Poggio al Moro

Vitelleschi palace (XV century)

THE NATIONAL MUSEUM

Entering the town from the Porta Maggiore (or Porta della Valle) through Cavour Square, probably the Etruscan former glory of the city does not seem evident.

On the left, the magnificent Vitelleschi palace (fifteenth century), built by the Archbishop Giovanni Vitelleschi between 1436 and 1439, and seat of the National Museum of Tarquinia, since 1924 has kept the Bruschi-Falgari collection, and the Civic Museum's archaeological finds.

The facade is divided into two sections: the lower one is smooth, with a portal in Renaissance style, and three windows. The upper section is an ashlar-work, on different levels. It is embellished with a one light window, an open gallery, three different kinds of mullion windows with two lights and, on embossed levels, it is also decorated with three splendid, gothic three lights windows adorned with spiral pillars and various, fine rose-windows.

Inside the Vitelleschi palace, after an imposing entrance-hall with cross vault ceiling, a beautiful courtyard with an octagonal

Terracotta urn in different colours (VI-V century B.C.)
Horse between two youths

marble well, adorned with the Vitelleschi family coat of arms, welcomes the visitor.

On the right side there is a long arcade with pointed arches supported by columns. The columns hold an open gallery covered by a wooden roof. Both the arcade and the gallery have cross vault ceilings. At the far end of the right side there is a staircase of low and wide steps, allowing access to the upper floors by horse. In the courtyard, along the arcade, some stone finds are displayed: between them, tufa or limestone blocks (VII-V century B.C.), decorated with oriental patterns bas-relief. Divided into panels and fascias, they probably were decorations of the main entrances of tombs. Moreover, some sarcophagi, dated from fourth and third century B.C., can also be seen. The wide collection of sarcophagi is exhibited on the ground-floor rooms. In Tarquinia, workshops of local artists manufactured sarcophagi on marble in large quantities, probably in imitation of those produced in Graecia Magna and kept up in the city. Some are made of limestone (e.g. the Magnate sarcophagus, end of fourth century B.C.), or tufa (e.g. the Magistrate sarcophagus, second half of third century B.C.).

Tufa slab with decoration in bas-relief

Tarquinia's workshops were famous for this production of burial monuments, meant for local families or patricians from neighbouring towns. The most ancient examples show the dead laying under the angled cover (known as "architectonic type"), with the body turned and the head rest on the left. Towards the end of the fourth century B.C., the body of the dead was in a partly sitting position, with an obvious reference to the position taken by guests on tryclinium (*kline*) during the banquets. It refers directly to aristocratic power. Reliefs or some paintings are just on one side of the sarcophagus: it has suggested that it was leaned against the wall of the tomb. A sarcophagus is decorated on all four sides with hunting scenes: a man between two animals, and a wild boar between two youths.

Some sarcophagi of patrician families

On both the main sides mythological subjects less frequente. Usually, scenes of how the dead pass through the perils of underworld to reach the afterlife, and his badges are engraved on the sarcophagus's stone.

Towards the end of the third century B.C., a half-naked figure laying on the cover and wearing simply a cloak appears as main decorative pattern. In the last sarcophagi exhibited the facial expressions are more stressed and they seem to introduce to realistic portraiture. In some items it is evident a sort of satisfaction in representing the old age or the ugliness of the dead persons. Their flabby bodies refer to the so-called *obesus etruscus* model, quoted also by Catullo, one of the most important Roman poets (87-55 B.C.).The sarcophagi shown on the ground-floor of the Museum come from the tombs of the main aristocratic families.

The Magistrate or Laris Pulenas *sarcophagus*
(III century B.C.)

Probably the best-known sarcophagus of the *Pulenas* family is the "Magistrate" one. The deceased is portrayed with a roll in his hands: a long Etruscan inscription shows his status and past

The Magnate or Velthur Partunus sarcophagus (IV century B.C.)

religious offices. The handmade work on local stone dates back to second half of the third century B.C.. A beautiful sarcophagus is that of the *Partunus* family, known as the "Magnate" one.

It is a refined marble work (end of the fifth century B.C.). On the coffin mythological scenes have been carved. On the main side and on the short ones, there are scenes of fighting Amazons. On the back side, scenes of fights between Centaurs and Lapites.

Very remarkable items are the sarcophagi of the *Alvethna*, *Pumpu* and *Camna* families. Especially, the *Ramtha Apatrui* one, decorated with the dead woman outstretched on the cover and with a sea-monster half human, half fish. On the case (first half of the third century B.C.) there have been carved *Scylla* and *Vanth*, the Etruscan goddess of Death.

Of great importance is a fragment of a stele (seventh-sixth century B.C.) adorned with two warriors in bas-relief.

In room 1, on the first floor, are displayed objects of the Villanovian period (between the tenth and the eight century B.C.), from the town of Villanova. This civilisation which was present in Campania and Emilia Romagna too, was wide spread in ancient Etruria. Its peculiar features are the small necropolis that had been built to the east of the tufa hill where the present Tarquinia stands. During the Villanovian period there were not urban settlements, but villages where the hut of the leader of the clan, obeyed and respected, was in the centre of it. The main burial rite was the cremation, as shown by the biconical cineraria, in form of a helmet (for men) or a bowl (for women). There have been found hut shaped cinerary urns too. As a rule the funerary equipment includes fibula, bronze razors, tripods, swords made of bronze, vases, pins (male tombs), and fibula, clasps, fusaroles (female tombs).

In rooms 2 and 3, on the first floor, objects inspired by Oriental designs, show how the Etruscan culture had been opened to contacts with other civilizations bordering the Mediterranean sea: Egypt, Cyprus, Rhodes, Syria. This Oriental period enjoyed a flourishing maritime trade for Tarquinia. Room 2 exhibits the Boccoris tomb burial furnishing: vases made in Tarquinia, ivory necklaces portraying Egyptian goddesses, situla (votive vase) decorated with religious scenes in honour of the Pharaoh Boccoris, and with black slaves, handles of lotus shaped bronze vases. Boccoris (according to Greek opinion) was the Pharaoh Bokorinef of the Egyptian twenty-seventh dynasty (second half of eighth century B.C.). These items have allowed as to date the tomb and the equipment from the beginning of the seventh century B.C. when the earlier Oriental influence in Etruria and Tarquinia had been documented.

In room 3 there are other Oriental articles; two ostrich eggs decorated with scarabs, bronze appliques made in Greece, alabasters, Assyrian griffon protons made of bronze. As for Egyptian and Phoenician culture, ostrich eggs and scarabs had an apotropaic importance to dispel evil spirits.

Jar on a high pillar   *Situla of faïence*

Tomb of Boccoris
(Second half of the eighth century B.C.)

In room 3 there are some ceramic items made in Tarquinia, painted in Geometric style, borrowed designs from Greek pottery. On the first floor, room 4, there is displayed the whole pottery collection, in chronological order.

The word *bucaro* comes from Hispano-portuguese, and in the 1700s and 1800s was the name of a particular type of ceramic objects from South-America, similar in style to the Etruscan one. *Bucchero* is now used to indicate a special typology of pottery.

The former Etruscan bucchero was made in Etruria in the seventh century B.C., during the Orietalizing period. This specimen is known as "thin" thanks to the delicacy and refinement of the vase's body. One century later, a "heavier" bucchero was produced.

Statues made of bronze (4th century B.C.)

Today, the craftsmen in Tarquinia are able to reproduce buccheri similar to the original Etruscan ones, perhaps more beautiful, feeding a large international market of "fakes made by genuine masters". In room 4, Etruscan-Corinthian vases made in Tarquinia (620-570 B.C.) are displayed. Coming from other areas of ancient Etruria there are several jars painted by the Etruscan Micali's painter, a little terracotta urn (sixth-fifth century B.C.) with scenes portraying youths and horses, a collection of protocorinthian vases (end of the eighth century-beginning of the seventh century B.C.), and painted pottery from Greece.

The Greek pottery found in Etruscan tombs, specially in Tarquinia's, gives tangible help in knowing better the Hellenic art. In fact, the most important collection of Greek pottery is displayed in museums of Etruscan civilization.

In room 5, on the first floor, there are exhibited vases decorated with Greek "blackfigured" style. The painter made a sketch using a punch on the vase, then he painted it in black silhouette. The paint was produced by a combination of powdered clay with iron oxide and sodium or potassium carbonate. The artist touched up the drawings with red ochre or white clay. Finally, with a special instrument of wood or bone, he carved the anatomical details and the robes upon it.

In this room there are displayed archaeological finds from archaic period (550-475 B.C.), articles of Rhodian, Ionic, Corinthian and Attic manufacture, coming from Greece.

From the earlier period, there are amphoras (storage jars) with horse proton painted in profile, or with a siren (590-580 B.C;). A goblet made by the painter known as *Xenocles* dates back to 560 B.C..

The big amphora of *Psiax* dates from

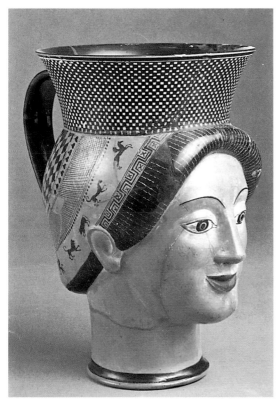

Jar of Karinos (510-500 B.C.)

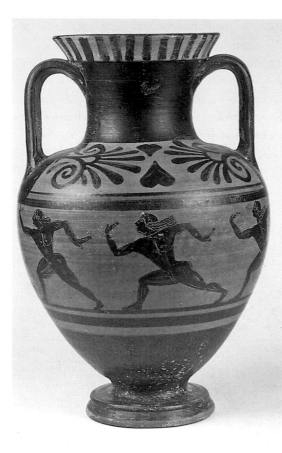

Blackfigure vase (V century B.C.)

520 B.C.. A little amphora in the black-figured style shows on its neck the fight between Apollo and Heracles for the tripod. It is the work of the well known ceramist *Nikostenes*. In the same room, there are seven amphoras ascribed to the painter known as *Antimes* (530-510 B.C.). There are also several amphoras called "E group" (540-530 B.C.). A vase of a certain importance for the use of a mixed technique (blackfigured style and redfigured style) is the Dionysos's one (510-500 B.C.). The Attic amphoras in blackfigured style, two of the most magnificent discovered, show the Caledonian boar-hunting of Heracles (560-550 B.C.), and the fight between Dionysos against two groups of warriors (530 B.C.).

The so-called *Sòstratos Anchor* is a portion of a marble anchor stock of 2.5 metres. It bears a Greek inscription, on Doric dialect in Egina characters. The manufacture probably belonged to the famous merchant of Egina, *Sòstratos*, quoted by Erodoto because of his riches, amassed thanks to international trade.

The epigraph dates back from the end of the sixth century B.C.. In rooms 6 and 7 on the first floor is displayed the red-figured pottery of the classical period, that is usually divided into sub-archaic phase (475-470 B.C.) and the phase influenced by the severe and classical Greek styles (460-300 B.C.).

Kylix (detail of black figures)
Fight between Ercole and Tritone (570-560 B.C.)

In comparison with the blackfigure one, the redfigure pottery allows a better artistic result: the details are not still scratched as a graffito on the black background, but painted on the red clay surface.

On the main side of an Attic redfigure amphora there is depicted the fight between Heracles and Apollo for the tripod of Delphi. It is ascribed to *Phintias* (510-500 B.C.).

A notable Attic black-figure vase, in the form of a woman's head, is a work of the ceramist *Karinos* (510-500 B.C.). A very effective bell-shaped Attic krater bears the rape of Europa. It is ascribed to the painter of Berlin (480-470 B.C.). A kylix (goblet) of Oltos shows a general meeting of Olympus gods. On its base there is scratched a dedication in Etruscan to the Dioscuri (510-

The rape of Europa
Attic stamnos by "painter from Berlin" (500-490 B.C.)

500 B.C.). A redfigure krater made by *Kleophrades* (500-490 B.C.) shows a gymnasium. An other notable Attic redfigure *kylix* bears Busiride pouring the wine into a glass raised by Phoenix. It is attributed to *Brygos* or *Duoris* (beginning of the fifth

century B.C.). The inside of a redfigure *kylix*, ascribed to *Epictetos* (510-500 B.C.) shows a naked silenus (according to the mythology, a human being with horse ears, tail and hooves) holding a leather bag full of wine.

A redfigure krater, attributed to the school of *Polignoto* (440-430 B.C.), shows a banquet with male participants.

Room 8, on the first floor, is dedicated to the Hellenistic period. There are some typical objects of Etruscan manufacture. The items are heterogeneous: redfigure vases from Tarquinia (sixth century B.C.), black overpainted ceramics, goblets from Megara (a town near to Corintho isthmus), ceramics without colours (second-first century B.C.), bronzes from Archaic to Hellenistic period, Etruscan jewels, Roman and Etruscan objects in bone or ivory, a small collection of Roman and Etruscan coins, some item coming from a votive stipis recovered near the temple of **Altar of the Queen** (terracotta votive offerings in human shape).

Several bronze *umboni* (reliefs in the middle of a round shield dodging sword-cuts) hold a great interest. In the main external side there are protons having the shape of animals or Acheloos

Votive head

heads (end of sixth century B.C.). Concerning the luxury articles, the most numerous are the mirrors, but there are other gold ornaments, as necklaces for example. Items of the Hellenistic period are collected in room 9. Here, is placed the masterpiece of the Tarquinian choroplastic: the two Winged Horses, an alto-rilievo from the decoration of the Altar of the Queen temple (sixth-third century B.C.).

On the second floor of the Museum, there are exhibited some tomb paintings, taken from the former places to preserve them better.

The most ancient paintings come from the Tomb of Olympiads (520 B.C.).

Winged horses (IV century B.C.)

At the back of the room, between a dummy door, scenes of dancing have been painted. On the left side there are displayed a two-wheeled chariot race and a boxing-match, that are in very bad condition. On the right side the games go on with three runners, a jumper, a discobolus and, very ruined, a scene of the Etruscan cruel game known as *Phersu*. On the tympanum there is a symposium with two men.

Tomb of the Olympiads - discobolus - (520 B.C.)

The Tomb of Bigas (490-480 B.C.), called also Stackelberg after the German archaeologist who found it in 1827, was probably painted by an Etruscan pupil of a Greek master. It was a luxury tomb, also in the interior finishing, but it suffered from the removal of the paintings from the walls. The decoration is displayed on two superimpose bands. On the lower one, the most conventional, there are painted banquets and dances. On the upper one, there are shown funeral games: this was the only time all the games known in Greece had been painted, and the typical Etruscan game of *Phersu*. In wooden galleries, with roof and curtains, there is a large audience both males and females, talking lively. Under the galleries there are painted some slaves talking and laughing.

Probably the best-known tomb in Tarquinia is the Tomb of Tryclinium. Its paintings show a banquet of three newly-married couples with attendants, on the back wall. On the left wall, young men and girls are dancing led by a cithara player. On the right wall, the dancers are accompanied by a flautist. Between the figures there are some birds, or little animals. A spray of ivy, following the outline of the fronton at the back wall, defines the different scenes.

Tomb of the Tryclinium
Detail on the right wall

Tomb of the Tryclinium
Details

A tomb of wide interest is the Tomb of Funeral Couch, whose decorations date from 460-450 B.C.. Some authorities have suggested that this tomb and the Tryclinium are both works of the same artist. Against this, it is argued that the stylistic differences are too marked to confirm that theory. Anyway, the Greek art has left a great mark on both. An impressive catafalque, surmounted by two conical headgears, is depicted on the back wall.

Under a tent two different funeral couches are painted, the so called *prothesis*, for two distinct dead persons. Then, the typical banquet is displayed, with three *klinai*, one at the bottom and two on the lateral walls. Outside the tent, the usual dances and funeral games are exhibited; small stylized trees with festoons are painted in the background. The upper part of slopes is chequered. The main roof-tree is covered with a thick vine pleaching, and circles.

The Tomb of the Black Sow dates from the middle of the fifth century B.C.. The frescoes show a deep feeling for beauty and symmetry. On each *klinai* (three on the back wall, and one on each side) are displayed one lying male couple, servants, and a cithara player. On the left side two women are dancing. On the right side a knight armed with a lance is led by a man and a dog. Probably this is a hunting scene. In fact, on the back tympanum there is painted a boar hunt.

The Ship Tomb dates from the middle of the fifth century B.C., too. However, it shows a stronger archaic influence. Its name comes from the big ship, full of sailors, painted at the beginning of the left wall. It is the witness of the past prosperous sea trade of Tarquinia, and it also refers to the activity of the dead.

On the back wall the typical banquet scene is depicted, with a couple of guests on each *klinai*, servants, a flautist and a cithara player. Dancing scenes, in poor condition, are painted on the entrance wall and on the right one.

The Bruschi Tomb, that is to say the gens *Apuna* one, dates from the second century B.C.. It has not been completely rebuilt.

Tomb of the Ship (V century B.C.)
Details of back wall

Scenes are displayed on a frieze decorated with dolphins.

On the entrance wall a woman, having a pomegranate (in the Ancient Rome it was a symbol of marriage) in her hand, is looking at herself with admiration in a mirror hold by a maid servant. Behind her, a trumpet player leads three men, the first of them on horseback. An other procession, on the back wall, is taking leave of a woman.

The motive of life after death is shown again on the left wall, where a third procession is followed by demons. At the beginning, two pillars support the ceiling: a woman and Charon, the ferryman of dead people, are painted there.

THE MONTEROZZI NECROPOLIS

The necropolis, dated from the ninth and eighth century B.C. (located in the hills surrounding the Civita and in the Saint Savino valley), indicates that the main burial rite at the time of Etruscans was the cremation. Inside the numerous well-tombs were placed the urns, specially the biconical ones and, rarely vases in form of huts. The most likely explanation for this different ceremony of burying the deceased's ashes is that the sex of dead influenced not only the form of the cinerary urns (helmet for men, bowl for women) or the funerary equipment, but also the ceremony itself. However there have not been found differences based on wealth or social background. It has been suggested that the Etruscan one was almost an egalitarian society.

The Tarquinia's necropolis are distributed over a large area all around the ancient city, today known as Monterozzi necropolis (where tombs are more numerous), Knoll of Quarter of Arches, Knoll of Hangman, Knoll above Selciatello, Selciatello knoll, Gallinaro knoll, Knoll of little horse, Quagliere knoll, Knoll of Perazzetta, Cretoncini knoll, The Roses.

The tombs, reveal the changes in social structure over time. An increase of burials and tomb furnishings show differences between social classes (it seems armies for men or jewels for women as marks of distinction). A huge quantity of ceramics or bronze articles inside the tombs, both from Etruria or Sardinia, perhaps from Greece and Central Europe, has been found.

The decorated tombs express the deep socio-economic change within the Etruscan world with increasing trade in Mediterranean area. Foreign painters (specially Greek-oriental ones) and craftsmen provided an example for Tarquinian art schools to follow, affected their way of working. In Monterozzi there are located the former painted tombs. There are almost two-hundred tombs with wall-paintings on six-thousand found in Tarquinia and its environs, and really numerous in Calvary and Second Arches areas.

Even if tombs of different periods are closely located without chronological order, burials similar in period or style (or painted in the same workshop) sometimes are nearby. The power and wealth of aristocratic class at that moment is shown with beautiful wall-paintings, and not with magnificent tombs. Frequently, the tombs are very small. The best examples of this production dates back to 530 B.C..

At that time, a large quantity of good Attic ceramics reached Tarquinia: the funerary equipment documents this state.

Tomb of the Augurs
Phersu, the executioner

Only few tombs can be seen. As time passed, habitual visiting, sometimes without any protection, have obliged the staff in charge to take the necessary measures. The tombs are now protected from excessive light with heavy glass sheets and visitors are allowed to go into the tombs in groups with alternate visiting hours. Then, there have been excluded from the sightseeing tour the tombs with the most damaged frescoes. The number of the tombs that can be seen have been reduced.

The main ones are listed here.

Tomb of Anina family
*(second quarter of the third century-first half
of the second century B.C.)*

This is the tomb of the aristocratic family known as *Anina*. The founder of the family *gens Larth Anina*, who according to his epitaph, saw that six sarcophagi, for himself and his relatives, would be ready.

Anina Tomb
Back wall

The inscriptions carved upon the sarcophagi and walls show the number of depositions about the members of the patrician clan, for three successive generations. The tomb is a big, quadrangular room, with smooth ceiling and a U shaped platform, articulated on three steps and set against the wall.

On it, there are hollowed out or leaned sarcophagi made of different materials (tufa, limestone and terracotta). The portraits of the deceased are sometimes carved upon the cover, outstretched on the *kline*, during the ritual banquets over which they presided.

Larth Anina ordered to be painted on the sides of the door two Etruscan demons of Death: *Charun* (Charon) and *Vanth*. The first one has an hammer in his hand to inflict punishment on the souls of deceased, the second one has a torch to light the journey during after-life.

Tomb of the Augurs
(second half of the sixth century B.C.)

This tomb is one of the most important monuments of the Etruscan painting in Tarquinia. The decoration, around all the

Tomb of the Augurs
The wrestlers

Tomb of the Augurs
Back wall

walls, is focused on the back wall where, on the sides of a closed portal, two hieratic male figures are painted. The first people to discover this tomb have suggested that the two men were
Augurs (that means the name of the tomb), personages of great
importance for Etruscan religion, painted in farewell pose.

The decoration shows funeral games and the past activities of
deceased. The scenes have not only an artistic value but also a
narrative vigour.

The main decorative aspect of the tomb is a description of a
wrestling game (that cover the better part of the right wall), a
very famous sport in ancient times. The painting shows the game known as *Phersu*, and one of the most bloody examples of
Etruscan justice. The judge is ready to give the starting-signal,
the spectators are waiting to see the fight and a sleeping slave,
perhaps in the wrestler's service, bear the essential features of
the game.

About the *Pershu* (the masked man), he was the executioner for the biggest crimes, which does not give great hope to the condemned man. In fact, completely hooded, he had to fight with a stick against a ravenous dog, set on him by the executioner. A little man painted on the left wall seems to assure that, in case of the convict winning, under discussion would be the fate of the executioner.

Tomb of the Bacchantes
(510-500 B.C.)

It was founded in 1874. There is a little quadrangular room, with a inclined, double slope ceiling. The *columen* is in relief and it has access from a *dromos* with steps.

Tomb of the Bacchantes
Married couple

The damaged paintings on the walls have their central point on dancers. The scenes are defined by little trees. The couple on the left side, perhaps the owner of the tomb and his wife, is important specially for the profiles of the heads. There are some crown pendent like small branches. On tympanum, lions and deer are struggling, and feline tracks are painted on entrance wall.

Tomb of the Baron
(last quarter of the sixth century B.C.)

It was called Tomb of the Baron after the Baron Stackelberg, who found it in the nineteenth century. The small room has a double slope ceiling, and around the walls there is a wide band in red, black and green colours.

Tomb of the Baron
Back wall

The frieze is fully coloured (white, black, red green and ochre) and the personages are set in geometrical order. The main scene shows two men and a woman. She is wearing a stylish tunic and a cloak and with raised arms she seems to be greeting a bearded man on the left, covered by a black cloak. He is encircling the arm of a young flautist and holding a goblet in the left hand. A small branch defines the three figures and divides the men from the woman reaching the afterlife. Two men on horse back complete the scene. On the right wall there is an other group with two youths who are talking animatedly and putting the bridles on two horses. They are wearing short cloaks bordered with various colours and with bracelets on their arms. Even if the decoration shows unusual subjects, it reflects decorum and elegance, with a peaceful consideration of Death.

Bartoccini tomb
(530-520 B.C.)

Founded in 1959, the sepulchre dedicated to Superintendent Renato Bartoccini, consists of a central room with three side cells. All the rooms have a double slope ceiling. On the small fronton on the back wall there is the traditional banquet scene, with two male couples laying on *klinai*, waited upon by maids and servants. On the small fronton at the entrance wall two sea-horses have been painted.

In a side cell, on the small frontons of short walls there are fighting animals, and on the long ones there are crowns made of pomegranates and lotus buds.

This tomb is the biggest hypogeum painted in archaic period. Its complex plan distinguishes this tomb from the other ones.

The painter was a great artist and his work shows links to Tarquinian blackfigure pottery.

Bartoccini Tomb
Entrance wall

Tomb of the Biclinium
(fourth century B.C.)

It is a tomb with one room, found in the eighteenth century. Its wall paintings are known thanks to the drawings of J. Byres, almost accurate copies of original subjects, even if different concerning the style. On the right and left walls there are scenes of banquets with well decorated *klinai*. Couples of men and women are portrayed, with maids wearing a chiton and naked male servants. The drawings are kept at Würzburg, Bavaria.

It has been suggested that this tomb comes after the Tryclinium one, kept in the National Museum.

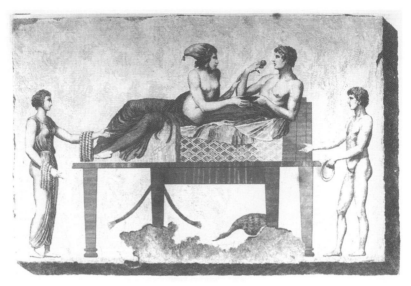

Tomb of the Biclinium
Woman with *tutulus*, man with *kylix* and an egg
(Sketch by J. Byres)

Tomb of the Biclinium
Woman with *rython*, man with *kylix*
(Sketch by J. Byres)

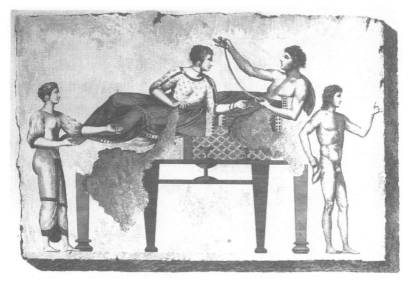

Tomb of the Biclinium
Man holding a taenia
(Sketch by J. Byres)

Tomb of Hunting and Fishing
(520-510 B.C.)

Discovered in 1873, this tomb is one of the most famous monuments of Tarquinia. It consists of two rooms, with double slope ceiling. Its name refers to graceful scenes portraying these activities painted on the small fronton of the first room and on the walls of the second one.

At the back wall of the first room is painted a scene with two riders coming back after hunting, with their catch and with servants. On the fronton of the entrance room is painted a banquet scene. On the walls, under coloured, narrow bands with pomegranates and lotus buds, there are some male characters, naked or wearing short loin-cloths, playing instruments or dancing. The background is defined by small trees with hanging crowns, cists, bandages and mirrors.

Tomb of Hunting and Fishing
Scene of fishing

In the second room, where the sepulchre was set, there is painted a couple during a banquet, with maids and servants. The walls are decorated with hunting and fishing scenes, in a seascape crowded by fishes and sea birds. Three fishermen in a boat

Tomb of Hunting and Fishing
The banquet

Tomb of hunting and fishing
The diver

are near a cliff where a young naked man is diving, cover the left wall.

On the back wall there is a boat with four men. One is fishing the stern, another is trying to hit a bird using a sling. A third boat and a hunter with a sling on a cliff are painted on the right wall.

Cardarelli tomb
(510-500 B.C.)

In the Monterozzi necropolis this tomb is dedicated to Vincenzo Cardarelli, the famous Italian poet born in Tarquinia. The tomb was found in 1959, but robbed and deprived of the funerary equipment. It has access by a *dromos* with steps.

It has only one quadrangular room, with double slope ceiling and *columen* in relief, decorated with rosettes and a spray of ivy coloured in red.

On the whole, the frescoes are well-done. In the semi-tympanum animals are shown: an the back walls tympanum, two groups with lions and gazelles; on the entrance walls, it can be seen a group with two birds and two leopards holding the *columen*.

All around the walls there are various human figures, defined by little trees with green-grey leaves.

The figures are well painted. On the back wall, on the sides of a false Doric door, with two wings and delimited by two piers, two flautists, or perhaps cithara players, wearing a jacket and a transparent tunic, are painted. On the sides of the door there is some pottery.

On the entrance wall, figures of athletes decorate the sides of the door. The artist shows a masterly and humorous intention in drawing their bodies and muscles in a grotesque way, and coloured of red. Groups of human figures cover the lateral walls. On the right side, a man wearing a white loin-cloth is throwing the wine from on his goblet. This was an Etruscan famous game known as *kòttabos*. A boy with two vessels in his hands, is looking at the throwing. The left group is composed by a cithara player and a dancer.

On the opposite side, two other groups of men are defined by little trees. A woman, perhaps the deceased, is dancing with the head covered by a border of her cloak.

The outlines of her body can be seen through the transparent tunic. A very effective scene executed with a refined technique. The woman dancer is surrounding by a naked, young servant

Cardarelli Tomb
The *kòttabos* player
Kòttabos game, imported from the Greeks of Sicily, consists in throwing wine
into a metal jar shouting the name of his beloved; the sound produced tells
the player if his feelings are returned.

holding a flabellum and by a maid with a mirror in her hands.

On the opposite wall, there are just two characters: a male figure wearing a loin-cloth holding a goblet; a flautist goes before wearing a crown and a cloak.

These paintings are ascribed to Tarquinian workshops of the sixth century. For their decorative style are similar to the Tomb of Bacchantes ones.

Tomb of Charons
(third-second century B.C.)

The tomb of Charons was been found in 1960, already robbed and deprived of funerary equipment. Its vestibule is higher than the other rooms, as noticed in a group of few tombs. It has access through a steep and curvilinear staircase. Against the walls of the rectangular vestibule, with a curved ceiling without *columen*, some viewing platforms have been provided. Two false Doric doors with two wings, coloured red, are carved upon the back wall and upon the right one. The geometrical ornament and reproduction of metal studs and wooden frameworks decorate the doors. They symbolise the entrance to the underworld and, ideally, the entry to the lower rooms where depositions are placed.

Two steep and uncomfortable staircases connect the rooms, holding the most part of the vestibule.

On the sides of the false doors Charons have been painted: it could be interesting to note that in the religious iconography the various demons are distinct by adding different appellatives to their names. The demons on the sides of the door at the back wall have blue skin and red wings.

The tunics are coloured in a different way: then, the right demon, wearing a double cloak, has a sword in his hands, the left one holds an axe.

The blue demons of the right wall wear red tunics. The demon on the left is covered by a cloak and has a winged hat, the other one wears a cloak. His hair is made of snakes.

Tomb of the Charons
Door with winged Charons

The paintings show accurate outlines. Concerning the tomb architecture dated back to the Hellenistic period, the tomb of the Charons distinguishes itself by for the beautiful false doors (there are similar ones at Norchia and Castel d'Asso).

Tomb 5636
(second half of the third century B.C.)

Found in 1969, it consists of a large sepulchral room with two epitaphs of family *Arnthunas* carved upon the walls. Unlike the other tombs, it has a flat ceiling; on the bases of the lateral walls and around the central pillar, marks of the sarcophagi are visible. The decoration, not unitary as may be found in the archaic and classical period, covers just the central pillar and the right wall. A winged Charon, big and menacing, with hair in the form of snakes and wearing a short tunic with cloak is painted on the pillar. A scene about the burial rite decorates the right wall. The deceased, led by a little boy and by *Vanth*, female demon holding a torch, reaches the entrance to the underworld. Charon, disguised as custodian of the World of Death, is seated in front on the deceased. To receive the dead there are two men, probably relatives predeceased.

Tomba 5636
Detail aus der rechten Wand

Tomb of the Lotus
(520 B.C.)

The tomb of the Lotus was found in 1962. It consists of a rectangular room with a double slope ceiling and four holes for supports on the left back side of the floor. It has access by a *dromos* with steps. The paintings are well-preserved, specially the ones on the back wall, where a panther and a lion and a big, polychromatic lotus flower decorate the wall. Both the flower and the animals are gaudy in an unnatural way. Under the frieze there is no ornament. The manufacture is ascribed to a workshop following Ionic style of decoration.

Tomba del Fiore di Loto
Der Löwe

Tomb of the Little Flowers
(second quarter of the fifth century B.C.)

Found in 1960, the sepulchre has a sloped ceiling. An ornament of rosettes and ivy decorates the central pillar. On the slopes, little red circles alternate with little flowers with three petal (that means the name of the tomb).

On the fronton on the back wall, two fighting-cooks are shown. The big frieze all around the wall bears the typical scene of the banquet, with music and dancing in an rural background. On the back wall a couple, outstretched on a *kline* well-decorated, enjoys the feast waited upon by two naked boys. On the lateral walls, women and men are dancing accompanied by the music of a flautist.

Tomb of the Little Flowers
Right wall

Tomb of the Flogging
(490 B.C.)

It was discovered in 1960. It consists of one rectangular room with double slope ceiling. There is a *dromos* with steps at the entrance. The paintings decorating the walls are damaged and their subject is not like that of any other tomb. In fact, the erotic matter is of great importance, specially in the two scenes on the left wall where there are four naked men, and two of them are whipping a woman. On the other walls scenes portraying fights of animals (panther and deer), dancers, one flautist and a boxer can be seen. The style of the paintings is Ionic (perhaps this work was made by the same workshop of the Tomb of the Bacchantes). The natural elements are few: it lays emphasis on human figures, both singles or in group, included in a magnificent structure focalised on the three false doors coloured by red.

Tomb of the Flogging
The flogger

Tomb of the Jugglers
(510 B.C.)

Discovered in 1961, it consists of a rectangular room, with double slope ceiling and false central *columen*. There is a long *dromos* with steps. The paintings, on the whole, are well-preserved, with the exception of the frescoes on the ceiling and on the entrance wall. The *columen* is red, as in most cases of the Tarquinian tombs.

The back wall bears the main scene. Under the tympanum, where a blue panther and a red lion are facing each other on the sides of the *columen* base, an elderly man (perhaps the deceased as a spectator or judge) with a long stick, sits on a stool, is looking at the show of three youths in his honour.

Tomb of the Jugglers
Back wall

Tomb of the Jugglers
The old man with the boy

The first boy, an acrobat with two baskets (perhaps to collect the game properties) at his foot, is throwing some disks to a graceful woman holding a candelabrum on her head. The girl, adorned with jewels, wears a long, transparent chiton showing her agile legs. A flautist, on the left, is accompanying the exhibition. Two little trees define the scene. On the left a naked boy seems to comment on with two children. A child is sitting on the ground, and the second one is standing on a platform, holding a crown.

On the sides of the entrance wall, few marks outline the figures of a boy and of a camel. On the right wall, a dance scene is shown: a syrinx player wearing a red cloak, is surrounded by two couples of female dancers. One of them has almost disappeared, two have blond hair. The girl with dark hair is the most interesting figure of the group, she is painted with an iconographic intention. Little blue leaves define the characters. On the left wall, are shown a naked boy with a raised arm, a male running figure with a *lagobòlon* in his hand; an old bearded man (perhaps a priest or the games promoter), held up by a young boy; big, black birds flying between different kinds of trees.

Finally, a man in the act of defecating finishes the wall decoration; behind him there is an inscription. It has been suggested that it may indicate the name of the painter. Perhaps it may have an apotropaic meaning. The trend of ornamental decoration is obvious in these paintings, with a special peculiarity in the bright polychromy.

Tomb of the Gorgòneion
(first quarter of the sixth century B.C.)

It was discovered in 1960. It consists of one quadrangular room, with a large and low platform all around three sides of the wall, the ceiling is double sloped with a *columen* in relief.

There is a *dromos* with steps. Unfortunately the paintings, even if almost visible, are faded. About the *columen* ornament, some traces of a red colouring can be seen.

On the fronton of the back wall, an evanescent proton of Gorgon (she gives the tomb her name) is painted in black, with the tongue and other particulars coloured by red. This portraying seems to suggest an apotropaic meaning, to repel bad luck: a similar example is present also in the Pulcella Tomb. A graceful frieze adorned with palmettes and opposite volutes decorates the sides of the Gorgon. On

Tomb of the Gorgòneion
Details

the same wall, under the frieze, two human figures are painted: two men are greeting each other waving their hands. They have a long crook, and wearing a bright tunic with bare shoulders and chest. Some birds perching on a little tree divide the characters. Other little trees embellish the walls of the tomb and the door jambs. They are decorated with emerald-green or blue leaves and red or brown berries (but the coloured pellicle of several parts is damaged). Numerous blue birds (perhaps pigeons) are flying or are perching on the trees. On the two entrance semi-tympanum, other volutes are painted.

Tomb of the Warrior
(last decade of the fifth century B.C.)

This sepulchre was found in 1961. Some platforms are set all around the walls. On the back wall, fighting-cocks and two panthers are painted. On the small fronton of the entrance wall,

Tomb of the Warrior
Left wall

there is shown a naked winged genie with a panther.

Scenes of a banquet and funerary games (athletic or acrobatic, musical or wrestling games) in honour of the deceased cover the wall.

On the back wall two couples enjoy the feast lying on the *klinai*, accompanied by music and waited upon by female servants.

On the left wall are painted funerary games, showing a discobolus, a javelin thrower, two boxers and a young flautist. A second flautist is accompanying the dance of an armed warrior (it means the name of the tomb), painted on the entrance wall, on the right. On the left side of the door, there are a chariot, a young naked athlete, a feline and a young horseman. The right damaged wall bears an armed knight and a foot-soldier.

Tomb of the Lionesses
(520 B.C.)

This tomb was discover in 1874, in Monterozzi necropolis. It consists of one rectangular room with double slope ceiling and inclined walls. The back wall was hollowed to form a small niche, perhaps to place a cinerary urn. To reach the tomb, there is a *dromos* with steps. With the exception of the entrance wall, the paintings are well-preserved. The tomb looks like a pavilion with its painted pillars (similar to the Tarquinian wooden ones), on the four corners and at the centre of the lateral walls, and with its slopes adorned with checked ornaments, like a tile roof. Bandages, red and green painted crowns are hanging down all around the walls.

The name comes from two opposing lionesses, painted on the back wall, on the sides of the *columen*.

Under the fronton, a bright krater with volutes and an ivy garland embellish the wall.

On the right, there is an *oinochòe*, and a utensil to draw off water or wine.

On the sides of the krater two musicians are painted, a flautist

Tomb of the Lionesses
Two dancers

and a chitara player. On the left, there is a female dancer wearing
a long tunic adorned with little flowers, a cloak, a hat and boots.
At the right end of the same wall, there is a couple of dancers, a
man and a woman. The girl with brown hair, is wearing a transparent tunic, the blond naked boy holds in his hand an *oinochòe*.

The niche is set in axis with the krater, under the vase. The
miniaturist decoration inside the niche shows a banquet in honour of the deceased. The paintings of the entrance wall are very
damaged. On the two semi-tympanum it can be seen traces of
sea-animals, perhaps sea-horses. On the lateral walls are shown
scenes from a banquet. On the right a couple of men, wearing

Tomb of the Lionesses
The female dancer

crowns are lying on cushions. One of them holds an egg and a *kylix* in his hands. On the left, an other outstretched couple, are holding a crown and a small branch. At the foot of the man on the right, there is a naked slave standing on a stool, holding a flute and an other object, perhaps a ring. The base of the tomb, that is usually monochrome, in this case is festooned with a graceful sea ornament. Dark-blue waves and dolphins in pairs of alternate colours, with flying birds.

An other frieze shows lotus flowers and palmettes, with a garland of green-leaves on the top. The above-quoted banquet does not seem to be a funerary one, but it is a symposium, a moment of aristocratic daily life, a socialisation rite. In fact, there are no

Tomb of the Lionesses
The banqueter holding an egg symbol of life

Tomb of the Lionesses
Details on the right wall

dead people, or symbolic doors to reach the underworld. And the big krater is not a cinerary urn, probably it is a vase for wine as the utensil depicted on the right may suggest.

From a stylistic point of view strong Greek-oriental influences can be seen concerning the frieze decorated with palmettes and flowers and the people at the banquet showing receding profiles and transparent robes. The dancers are smaller in dimension and qualitatively very good, specially the dancing symmetrical couple.

The polychrome shows a very effective contrast between the colours, and their variety is wider than usual. The Tomb of the Lionesses is very similar to the Tomb of the Augurs, the Tomb of the Inscriptions and the Tomb of the Jugglers, which may share the same artist. A comparison with the Tomb of Hunting and Fishing has been suggested concerning the maritime frieze of the base.

Tomb of the Leopards
(480-470 B.C.)

Attic vases of the funerary equipment missing during the discovery period are now kept in Baltimore, Frankfurt and Hildesheim museums.

The tomb, found in 1875, consists of one room, with a double slope ceiling and an entrance *dromos* with steps (the actual decoration is not the former one).

The paintings show huge lacunas with the exception of the tomb's posterior part.

The ceiling is completely well-decorated: also the central *columen* is adorned with rosettes and concentric circles of different colours, the slopes show a checked polychrome ornament.

On the tympanum of the back wall, on the sides of a little tree, two opposite leopards (they give the tomb their names) show up on their bright background painting with dark spots. Behind them on the corners, little trees are painted.

Under the frieze, on the same wall, a scene of ritual banquet in honour of the deceased is shown: three couples (two mixed and a male one) wearing crowns on their heads are outstretched on well-decorated *klinai*, waited upon by naked slaves. The first man on the right holds in his hands a big metal goblet and a ring (perhaps used for a game).

Under and behind the *klinai* small trees embellish the scene. On the entrance wall, poor coloured traces of the former tympanum decoration can be seen, but on the left side of the door, a dancer is still visible. On the right side, some pottery is visible.

The ornament of the lateral walls is full of different personages and natural elements. Dancers, flautist and cithara players cover the right side, defined by small trees with berries and leaves. A procession consisting of six people is advancing at the back: there are four servants holding pottery for drinking, headed by two musicians, a cithara player and a flautist. These figures also defined by trees. Marks of the carved sketches and

Tomb of the Leopards
The people at the banquet

Tomb of the Leopards
Detail of a young man with Kylix

guide-lines are still visible. The fame of this tomb is greatly superior to the real artistic quality of its paintings, even if they have been made by an Etruscan good painter, but bereft of stylistic subtleties.

The component outlines are conventional and the drawing line is not of high quality. The characters are rigid and out of proportion. However the chromatism is lively, showing effective contrasts. There can be seen a marked difference between the ornaments of the lateral walls: the right side shows lively musicians and dancers, the left one bears a procession of servants. Concerning the people at the banquet at the back, the ones on the right side do not seem as good as the others.

Tomb of the Leopards
The musicians

The style may be defined as archaic, but with strong Attic influences, as the monumental structure and gigantic figures could suggest. However, these influences have been interpreted by the Etruscan artist in a popular-like manner, as regards to the later Tomb of Tryclinium, painted by a Greek master.

Tomb of Orcus
(end of the IV beginning of the III and the II century B.C.)

It can be considered the most important monument of the Etruscan plain during the Hellenistic period, and it was discovered in 1868.

Vincenzo Cardarelli, a poet from Tarquinia, wanted to show in this tomb the beauty of a face raised from death. He wrote:

Alto su rupe
battuto dai venti, un cimitero frondeggia:
cristiana oasi del Tartaro etrusco.
Là sotto è la fanciulla
bellissima dei Velcha,
che vive ancora nella Tomba dell'Orco.[1]

It is composed of two linked sepulchral rooms (Orcus I and Orcus II) that had been modified later on. The original ornamental themes are missing, their disappearance suggests a gloomier and more dramatic idea of death.

Emphasising the representation of many mythological Greek characters (Aiax, Tiresias, Persephone, Theseus), it highlights the pathetic figure of a young man, somebody believes he is Ipnos the God of Sleep on purpose situated among the main characters of the funeral banquet. In this painting gold plates show off in a sumptuous way.

Representations of legendary heroes want to highlight the real human fight against the roles of afterlife. The concept of afterlife is regarded with fear, so as testify the decline of the an-

Tomb of Orcus I - Face of Velcha

cient Etruscans thoughts. In this paintings can be seen distrust, pessimism, ineluctability, desperation, in the place of optimism, or at least realism.

The sweet figure of a woman represents - if we take into consideration the noble title *Velcha* written on one side - the expression of the feminine Etruscan beauty and it can be considered an extreme attempt to leave evidences of it.

Tomb of Orcus II - Representation of Teseo

Tomb of the Pavilion of the Hunting
(end of the VI century B.C.)

Discovered in 1962 it consists of a room with a double sloping roof and a high platform, situated on the lateral and back walls with the insertion of four sockets for the feet of a funeral bed.

The sepulchre is very suggestive imagined as a pavilion for hunting, made of wooden framing, covered with material. The roof, realised in squares, is surrounded by a border of lions, stags, bulls, horses, dogs, horsemen and warriors. On the walls a view with hills, trees and a feeding deer is represented.

Tomb of the Pavillon of the Hunting
Roof and back wall

Tomb of the Panthers
(end of VII century B.C.)

Opened in 1971, this tomb was suddenly closed again. In 1987 it was re-opened after, restoration work. In this tomb, the ground of which is composed is gathered in block with small irregular stones. It consists of a tiny rectangular room with a double-sloping roof and two high platforms on the walls. The access is through a *dromos*, provided with stairs bearing a small cells on the left wall. Decorations are limited to the back wall and the hall. On the back wall there are represented two panthers (from which the tomb takes its name). They stand face to face with front legs raised.

On the entrance wall, on both the door sides, there are represented two crouched panthers. Their bodies, in black and red colour, are evidence of a phase in the history of these paintings called "Orientalizing", that is to say before the "Ionic phase". This style is attested, until today, only in centres like Cerveteri and Veio.

Tomb of the Panthers
Back wall

Tomb of the Shields
(end of the IV century B.C.)

Discovered in 1870, it is a big and complex Hellenistic hypogeum provided with four openings: one in the central position and linked to two rooms at the back, and two others on the sides linked through doors and windows, decorated with a painted frame.

Different scenes are painted on the entrance wall, but the complex in its whole represents members of the aristocratic family *Velcha*, owner of the sepulchre. On the entrance wall can be seen a young woman playing tibia and another playing a trumpet. They are accompanying the *processus magistralis* of *Laris Velcha*, the founder of the tomb, followed by members of the family and *lictors*.

On the back wall a banquet with *Larth Velcha* half-lying on his bed with his wife *Velia Seitithi* giving him an egg is represented.

Tomb of the Shields
Velthur Velca with his wife Ravnthu Aprthnai

She is well dressed, like every other people from the same social position, she sits next to her husband's feet as was habitual.

Not far from them there are the two other members of the family, *Vel* and *Arnth*, *Larth*'s grandparents, standing and wearing large cloacks. Over the windows winged geniuses, symbols of the family, show up. On the right side of the door there is a naked servant, a man and two women.

On the left wall there are represented *Velthur* and *Ravnthu* one more time, but this time they sit on folding stools. The man holds a sceptre, symbol of his power.

The room at the back has walls decorated with many big golden shields, ornamented, carrying the inscription from which the tomb takes its name.

Tomb of the Typhoon
(middle of the II century B.C.)

Belonging to the noble family of *Pumpu*, it is one of the biggest of the entire necropolis. Discovered in 1832, we can enter through a long corridor provided with stairs on which are located the sarcophagus. Some of them are still present on the site.

The ornament is constituted of decoration on the walls, with dolphins jumping on the sea surface. In the centre of the left wall, under the control of two demons, there is a procession of judges, apparently going to hell, accompanied by a melancholy group of *lictors* and musicians.

On every side of the central pillar a huge winged monster the Typhoon from which the tomb takes its name representing a telamon (that is the support of the whole structure). It has a human face and a human body but his legs, from the knees, consist of snakes. The painting shows a good artistic taste, with prospective light and shade effects, mainly because of crowding figures and the position, on different levels, of the heads of the members. These figures are evidence of the ready-to-be-established Roman art. In fact they seem to be a transition sign of the exhausted Etru-

Tomb of the Typhoon - Detail from the central pillar

scan culture in favour of that of Rome. Now afterlife is like Typhoon: it is mysterious, it terrifies and sentences to a terrible life, with no protection.

The colourful inscriptions in Latin, on some plates, give an idea of the huge conceptual change compared to the glorious centuries.

Tomb of the Bulls
(beginning of the second half of the VI century B.C.)

Since its discovery (1892), it is considered one of the oldest decorated tombs in Tarquinia. Following discoveries in the necropolis show this tomb has to be considered among the most important documents attesting the vitality of the parietal pain-

Tomb of the Bulls
Bull against homosexuals

tings - and of the Greek oriental original art as well - that is for the mythical nature of the representations as well as for the obscene nature of some figures around.

The prominent motive is a mythical character situated between the two doors of the funeral rooms, in which it is represented the trap of Achilles to Troilus. All around there, there is an exotic, oriental vegetation, with a big palm right in the middle of the painting. The entire architectonic decoration of the rooms is interesting and elegant. On the right a semi-tympanum, a bull from which the tomb takes its name, runs after a horseman. In the hall there are scenes of the sea in very bad condition.

What is attractive for the visitors are the representations of erotic groups that, for some experts, can be interpreted as a contrast between the cruel reality of life and the ineluctability of death. Of interest is the representation of a homosexual scene with two men. In the funeral paintings of Tarquinia the man is usually

Tomb of the Bulls
Details with horseman Troilus

painted in red colour and the woman in white colour. The homosexuality is here represented in pink colour so to highlight its diversity.

Tomb of the Bulls
Details from the entrance wall

RELIGIOUS AND CIVIL MONUMENTS

Going along the left side of the Museum, we can see on the right, the Tower of Fani, surrounded by the Vitelleschi Palace; continuing we reach Piazza del Duomo, where S. Margherita Church is situated. It was raised to the status of Cathedral in 1435 by Eugenio IV, the Pope who proclaimed the reconciliation of the Greek Church with the Latin one.

The inside part of the Duomo is divided in one nave and two aisles and a vestibule that comes first. The presbytery, raised in 1761, preserves the original shape, with a gothic arch and a cross vault. Frescos, some very impressive, are to be attributed to Antonio da Viterbo, called "il Pastura", an artist who was very active

The Cathedral or Dome

in central Italy between the XV and XVI century and who was a disciple of Pinturicchio and Perugino.

In the left span is situated the Altare della Trasfigurazione, distinctive for the subject of the picture representing Jesus, situated on the Tabor mountain: it is a copy of the eighteen century of a painting made by Raffaello, but attributed, as many others in the church, to Luigi Boccanera.

The Bizantine Madonna, situated on the altar of the chapel and devoted to the Sacro Cuore, comes from the church of S. Maria in Valverde.

Considered to be prodigious, the Black Madonna (that is the name chosen by the villagers) was venerated in the past.

The present facade, dated back to 1933, is attributed to Pietro Magni, that replaced the old one in Baroque style.

Situated in the Duomo square, on the right side of the Cathedral, the tower on the ancient Palazzo Vescovile is still well preserved. On the other site, right on the back, almost behind the

Porta Castello

Duomo, can be seen a portico with a Torre Mozza next to it.

In front of the Duomo there can be seen some buildings from the XII and XIII centuries. The first on the left, clearly a Torre Mozza, preserves in its centre a beautiful round arch window with one light.

Along the street that links the Duomo with Porta Castello,

S. Maria in Castello and the tower

marking the southern border of Terziere di Valle, there can be seen some civil structures dated back to the XII and the XIV centuries. In the first building there are two arches (one is plugged) that belong to a portico. It is also possible that the building, built between the XV and the XVI century, could have been the seat of a bishop.

At the crossroads of Via di Porta Castello and Via della Cateratta, the small building on the corner was the seat of a hospital for men between 1470 and 1586. It is followed by a group of small houses, that in spite of recent enlargements, still preserve the same medieval architectural characteristics of the XIII and XIV centuries.

The street ends with a fortified door realised at the beginning of the XV century.

From Matilde comes its name, the Torrione in the walls whick dominates the sea.

The Porta Castello marks the borders of the medieval town, surrounded by walls made of tufa. In the vicinity of the Castello, owned by Matilde di Canossa (1046-1115), daughter of Bonifacio III, Marquess of Tuscany, and Beatrice di Lorena, a woman in possession of many estates in the north and central areas of Italy and Lotaringia.

After the grand complex of fortifications with a double door (one provided with a shutter and the other with a crank), the tower called Castello shows up in front of the monumental church of S. Maria in Castello, and on its left, that it is considered the highest of Corneto (43 mt). It probably was used as a reference point for travellers and sailors and for sighting as well. At the beginning, in this area the political, religious and strategic centre of the city was situated.

S. Maria in Castello, great example of roman-lombard style, was built starting from Christmas 1121. It was built with the money of both the civil power and the religious one, with the consensus of the citizens. Its construction ended a century later and in front of 10 bishops it was consecrated. It has the shape of a square and a facade provided with three portals with a mullioned window with two lights above it. The rose window is situated in a strange lateral position.

The inner part of the church is divided into one nave and two aisles along which there are nine polystyle pillars that end up with three apses. The dome in the centre of the church and the unique wind-shaped bell tower are not the originals, but recent restorations. At the beginning of the front nave there is an octagonal baptistry.

Important, but now almost disappeared, are the cosmatesque mosaics (that is they were realised by the school of Maestri Comacini, sculptors, architects, stonecutters, and bricklayers that, in the High Middle Ages, spread, not only in Italy, a wealth of magnificent architecture). They are situated on the ground and on the central door that once was well decorated.

In the XV century decay began. In 1566 were entrusted the Dominican Fathers with the church but it was soon unhallowed because a crime was committed in it. In 1572 was a temporary housing for soldiers and only in 1585 it was reconsecrated and given to the Franciscan Fathers who became its owners until the XIX

Hospital of S. Spirito, seat of the historical archive

century. In 1810 a Napoleonic decree abolished the religious orders and the church was closed, to be conceded later by Pope Pio VII (1816) to the female orphanage of Corneto. In 1849 the church was used as stabling for horses. Only in 1875 the Kingdom of Italy recognised the building as a national public monument. The repair work finished in 1969. Today the church is under cultural care and it is often used for conferences, concerts and weddings.

Walking along Via della Ripa we can see the elegant Torre Cialdi, and on the right, a characteristic building from the XIV century with a beautiful portal and two windows with two lights on the upper level. It is the elegant hospital of S. Spirito, the first city hospital (finished in 1447), today used as a historical archive.

The portal, whose moulding is an evidence of the Renaissance arrival, has two rectangular windows on the ground floor and, on the upper floor, two elegant mullioned windows with two lights, in Gothic style and connected to each other by a single window-sill.

A book, stored in the Historical Archive, is very important for a deeper knowledge of the Medieval society of Corneto. Its name is the "Margherita". Precisely, it consists of a very big register (32,8 x 51 cm), whose bookbinding goes back to 1789. It has a cover made of wood, covered with gold ornamented brown leather, carrying studs and buckles made of brass. It consists of a collection of notarial documents of a certain importance in the Repubblica Cornetana.

The "Margherita" is also called "Codice" and consists of 591 documents from 1201-1595. The beginning of the transcription of the *Codex* acts can be traced back to 1293.

The complex on the left side, has a tower of the XII century; the next building, from the XVI century, once was used as a foundling hospital. Today the adjacent church of S. Spirito, constructed in Baroque style and dated back to 1611, is abandoned.

The tower situated in the middle of the road, is one of the best preserved in the whole city, it is called Barucci. It shows muchre-

Church of S. Pancrazio

Church of S. Martino

storation work, some of it done in recent times.

In the square, on the left side, there is Palazzo Sacchetti, a building owned by the Sacchetti family and constructed during the Renaissance. At the front of the square there is the Torre del Drago, with an ashlar basement situated close to more recent buildings.

Going along Via delle Torri, on the left side, we see one of the most characteristic monuments of Corneto: the Palazzo dei Priori.

It is considered by some to be the old seat of the municipality, before the construction of the present Municipio which is still functioning. Others, on the contrary, think that the administrative activities were carried out in another building situated in Via degli Archi. It is possible that both the buildings carried out some administrative work, even if the presence of the church of S. Pancrazio in the neighbourhood makes the first solution be more possible. The Palazzo dei Priori was constructed in the XII century, gathering together many different buildings, so as to realise a bulky fortified structure. At present it is the seat of the Società Tarquiniese of History and Arts.

Other buildings overlooking the square can be traced back to the XII and XIII century, but the most prestigious element is the church of S. Pancrazio, whose construction is traced back to the end of the XI and XII centuries. The local historian Dasti considers it to be the place where Pope Innocenzo III met Pietro d'Aragona King of Navarra.

The church had been for centuries the centre of the religious and political power. It was the scene of subjugation acts made by Casato di Tolfa and Castel Sant'Angelo, and also of other criminal acts. It had been restored many times and stayed opened until the XX century. After that it was restored and used for exhibitions, conferences, concerts and consequently given to the Società Tarquiniese of History and Arts. The inside part has a unique four-sided plan. Luchino Visconti utilised it for his movie "La caduta degli Dei".

The Via degli Archi, which begins in Piazza S. Pancrazio, is one of the most suggestive of the town, because it maintains the same structure of a medieval town even if there are some changes from the XV century. Going along it we reach one of the meeting points of the medieval town, with architecture from the XII and XIII centuries: the Church of S. Martino.

Clearly of Roman style, S. Martino is probably the oldest church of Corneto still existing. Its existence can be traced back to 1051. It has always been a poor church because of the small number of its parishioners. Inside there are still traces of frescos

Church of the Annunziata

with the image of S. Anna and the Vergine Col Bambino dated
back to the XV century.

In the same area there is one of the most beautiful churches of
the town: l'Annunziata of the XII century and first dedicated to S.
Pietro Apostolo. Neglected for a long time, in 1667 it was utilised
as a place for meditation by a Captain of a French garrison. This si-

Church of S. Salvatore

tuation caused a reaction of the villagers and the religious authority opened it again. Nowadays it is under the care of the Suore della Carità.

On the left side, going along Via S. Giacomo, we reach, on the right, the small but very suggestive church of Salvatore, of the XII century, abandoned in 1665 and then finally deconsecrated.

The next coming church of San Giacomo is a Roman structure dated back to the XI-XII century. In 1570 it was already in a

Facade of the Palazzo Comunale

very bad condition. In the XVIII century it was consecrated for use as the chapel of the public cemetery. The inside walls were probably frescoed, but only some fragments are still visible.

Going back to the square in front of the Museum and going towards Corso Vittorio Emanuele from Piazza Cavour, immediately on the left, there is a small square where an octagonal well made of tufa is located. On its facades we can see the Vitelleschi coat of arms, and also images of Saints protecting Tarquinia: San Teofonio, San Lituardo, San Pantaleone e San Secondiano.

A statue made of bronze has been recently placed close to it. It is of a young lady, with wind swept hair lying under the sun. The name of the statue, which was a present (1990) to the town

Genealogical tree from Corito, founder of Tarquinia, to in order from the bottom: Corito, Dardano, Anchise, Enea, Ascanio, Silvio, Latino, Alba, Capi, Tiberino, Agrippa, Elladio, Aventino, Silvio, Proca, Amulio, Numitore, Romolo and Remo, *Frescos from the Palazzo Comunale*

by the author Emilio Greco to commemorate the local poet Vincenzo Cardarelli, is "Memoria dell'Estate".

The street linking the square of the museum to the next one, where in the XV century there was constructed the Palazzo Comunale, testifies, in the same period, interventions, sometimes original, that did not alter the street plan. Two serious epidemics brok out in a short period during the XVI century, drastically reducing the population of the town thus slowing its development.

The demographic decrease continued for the next two centuries and in 1872 the population of Corneto was only 2290 people but in the Etruscan Tarquinia they were 100.000 and even 35.000 in 1300.

The two Terziere "del Poggio" and "della Valle" were in such a bad state that Bishop Gaspare Cecchinelli (1630-1666) gave disposition to demolish every seriously damaged building. This caused a huge restoration and clearance operation. In the XVIII century new settings of the Piazza del Municipio were begun, more or less similar to the one we see today. There were built two new churches (S. Leonardo and La Madonna del Suffragio) that, with the third one existing at that time and demolished later (S. Maria Nuova), had to offer an elegant spectacular view with a fountain of drinking water in the middle.

In the XIX century the axis of Corso Vittorio Emanuele was prolonged and the church of S. Maria demolished so as to extend the street as far as the present Belvedere.

The Palazzo Comunale, built up in the XIII century, in Roman style and enriched with elements in Gothic style, was used as seat of the Civil Power in the place of other buildings utilised in the past. It was built along the urban wall. With the passing of time it was changed several times, even if some traces of the ancient structure are still visible.

Developing in a horizontal direction, in 1476 the Palazzo was seriously damaged because of a very bad fire that caused the destruction of many important documents preserved in the building. For its restoration work Donato Bramante, one of the greatest ever architects was appointed. Unfortunately the managers, in 1510 preferred to employ local constructors, probably for economic reasons. In 1512 Bramante requested restoration work activities but the administrators did not agree. In October 1534 (in the meantime Bramante died in Rome in 1514), the heads of the city decided to give the work to Antognetto, master builder.

The restoration works of the Palazzo had been executed in an unorganised way in the following centuries. Some restoration works, dated back to the XVI century, testifies that it was utilised as a theatre. At the end of the XVIII century, after a further period of negligence, a tier of boxes was replaced by a new gallery. Unfortunately in 1925 the building was in very bad condition and its closure was decided. Around the 1940s the theatre was finally demolished to be utilised for the realisation of the Sala Consiliare del Comune.

The external ornaments had been realised step by step. To the primitive uninterrupted arches of the facade, in the XVI, some changes were realised. The lodge realised before 1366 was at the beginning without stairs and covered, and it had only the balcony. The stairs were added later, provided with two arches transformed in round arches in the XV century. The cover was built in the XVII century.

The Torre Civica is a restoration work of the XV century. It is divided in two parts by two frames of nenfro. The lower part is also the one running along the windowsills of the other building. The four corners of the top-floor flat are highlighted by strong pilasters, modelled by couples of semi-columns that give to the whole building an idea of majesty.

In the rooms on the first floor there are some interesting frescos, restored in 1997 (as the back facade of the building). Of a major interest are frescos of a genealogical tree representing on the top Romolo and Remo, founders of Rome. It also shows some other mythological characters, among which the first one is Corito, founder of Tarquinia. Tarquinia's foundation was usually attributed to the twin.

In Matteotti Square the church of Suffragio begun to be built in 1750, during the second half of the XIX century it was closed because it was in very bad condition. It was opened again in September 1881 and in 1978 was fully repaired and preserved.

The facade, late-baroque, can be divided in two parts overlapped and separated by a broken thick frame: it consists of columns, one entry with a big arched window bearing a tympanum on the top.

The seven founders
Church of S. Leonardo

The elegant inside part, with one nave, developed on an apparently octagonal plane, is the result of a squared surface whose corners are hidden by walls.

A big inside door divides the entrance door from the hall and is characterised by paintings from the XVII century. One represents the miracle of S. Isidoro Agricola who makes water flow from the ground controlled by the Virgin with the Child. Another one represents S. Francesco da Paola, Giovanni Nepomuceno, Luigi Gonzaga, and Giuseppe Calasanzio. A third one represents the Madonna who receives prayers from the souls of Purgatory.

In the same square there is the church of S. Leonardo (or Dell'Addolorata or Chiesola) from the XVII century as well, and in a Baroque style. It was built in 1746 and restored in 1756. It was built on the ruins of old demolished buildings. Among them there was a temple dedicated to La Madonna dei Sette Dolori (Our Lady of the Seven Sorrows) from which the old church took its name.

When the religious orders were abolished in 1810 the church was turned into a barrack for the French army in 1813. Reorganised by Pio VII one year later, the religious people were able to have it back until 1897 when the monastery of Valverde, that came under the jurisdiction of S. Leonardo too, was abolished. Then, the church was abandoned. In 1931 it passed under the management of the Ministry of the Interior. In 1970 the building was repaired and given to the Fathers of Sacraments.

The elliptical disposition of the interior part, carried out by Navone, recalls the Sant'Andrea at Quirinale of Bernini, on the contrary the volumetric appendixes of the vestibule and presbytery seem to have been influenced by the Borromini del Sant'Agnese in Agone style. Then the horizontal structure seems to be a translation with the same motif as Sant'Ivo alla Sapienza.

Following via Dante Alighieri, on the right, almost in the middle, there is the church of SS. Trinità, built in the XVII and

Church of SS. Trinità

XVIII centuries in the place of a temple dating back to the XIII century. In the middle of the 1700s it was almost abandoned, to be closed in 1814 when, owing to the demolition of S. Maria Nuova, the Confraternita della Misericordia (Brotherhood of Mercy) moved to live there.

The church, at the moment, is not used for religious activities, except during the Holy Week, when it is occasionally opened to put in it the Cristo Morto (the Dead Christ) giving the name to the homonymous procession of the Venerdì Santo (Good Friday).

On the top of the climb, known as Via Alberata Dante Alighieri, on the highest part of the town, at the beginning of the 1980s a private citizen made to repair some rooms used as deposits for many centuries. He turned them into a library of international importance and provided a room for congresses with videoconferencing and simultaneous translation equipment.

Church and convent of S. Francesco

Crib from the XVII century
Church of S. Francesco

In there, now there is the Istituto per la Storia della Democrazia Repubblicana (Institute of Republican Democracy), an archive that contains documents about the different political parties in Italy from 1943. The entrance in now in the parallel street of Via dei Magazzini.

Climbing the hill of Porta Tarquinia we reach, after 100 metres, a square. On the left there are the church and the convent of S. Francesco, built between the end of the XIII and the beginning of the XIV centuries, on Roman style as testified by the beautiful central rose window of the facade. There is also a certain influence of Gothic style. Both of them had been built on the place where an older oratory, dedicated to the Holy Trinity, was erected. The cause of it seems to be a miracle of the Saint of Assisi. The church was from the very beginning owned by the Grey Friars.

S. Francesco had a certain influence in the religious and civil life of Corneto: several official acts were prepared and signed in this building. On the 23rd April of 1392 the municipal flag was consecrated there. In 1367 Pope Urbano V, coming back from Avignon, stayed there; in 1481 Sisto IV also spent some days there and in 1509 also Giulio II.

In 1435 Cardinal Vitelleschi gave as a present the relicts of S. Agapito, stolen from the city of Palestrina destroyed by his army.

The church, modified several times, is divided into a nave and two aisles. The inside part was altered nearly everywhere and, stayed unmodified only in the left aisle. Each nave has five spans. The chapels on the right were added between the XV and XVI century.

Along the left aisle there is a small chapel dedicated to Bonaventura di Bagnoregio.

In the apsidal chapel, behind the major altar, was buried Carlo D'Angennes dei Rombouillet, bishop of Mans and legate of Carlo IX at the Holy See, who was killed in 1587 in the Vitelleschi Palace. In the right apsidal chapel there are paintings representing S. Barbara, works made by Mola, a Roman mannerist, follower of Caravaggio.

Along the right aisle a small chapel is dedicated to Giovanni da Triora, martyr in China. After it there are the chapel of Immacolata and another one dedicated to S. Antonio. Then there is the very well considered chapel of Presepe (the Holy Crib).

The access to the very beautiful conventual cloister, with a renaissance well in the middle of a garden, is from the sacristy. The bell tower on the back is more recent (1612) but, possibly, it replaces another one wing-shaped provided with three bells - as in the church of S. Maria in Castello.

Continuing on from Piazza Matteotti through via Garibaldi towards the homonymous door, opened in 1932, on the right side there is Vipereschi Palace. In the inside part Urbano VIII (the Pope who condemned Galileo, because he argued against the Copernican system of the universe), made to function the so called "Ergastro" in 1627.

Palazzo Vipereschi

As reminded by a stone situated on the facade, today utilised by the University of Agraria, the "Ergastro" was a "Pia Casa di Penitenza" (or "Ergastolo") a prison for people in religious orders who had committed crimes. With this initiative they wanted to ensure that priests (and nuns), who had been convicted, were not put in common jails where they could have learned a bad language and other vices.

It consists of a big room on the ground floor and 60 cells on the upper floor. During the day the prisoners could move freely in the inside; during the night, on the contrary, they were forced to stay in their cells. The method failed, because somebody was still able to commit crimes inside, run away from the jail. New inquisitions and repression were brought in. Common people believed that once someone entered the "Ergastro" he was not able to go out, not even after his death.

The prison was repaired in 1728 and then closed after the annexation of Corneto to the kingdom of Italy in 1870. Garibaldi was one of its guests in 1882, when he was visiting Corneto. In the two upper branches, where there were the cells, are now used for the Guardia di Finanza (Customs Officers) and Carabinieri (Carabineers).

On the same side of the street there is the small chapel of the Cross, from the XIV century, in a pleasing Baroque style. The building (of the XV century) was the seat of Hospital for men from 1592 to 1918 and it was ruled by Fatebenefratelli.

Continuing towards Porta Garibaldi, on the right, there are the church and the monastery of the sisters Passioniste, built in 1771 after the demolition of the old structures in 1759.

During the repairing of some frescos in which there were paintings representing the Virgin and some Saints, the face of Maria appeared very pale, but suddenly turned to be coloured causing emotion and astonishment to the workers. The painting was so exposed for 12 years in the palace of the clerk of the works where it was venerated by the community as a series of miracles had been attributed to it. On the occasion of the consecration of the conventual church of the Passion, the image of the Virgin had been transferred to the main altar. From 1810 to 1814 the sisters were forced to leave the convent because of the Napoleonic decree that suppressed religious orders. In this period the building was transformed to an orphanage for girls, a school, and a public hospital for women.

In the monastery are preserved several paintings from the XVI and XVII centuries. In particular they are the Madonna and the

Church of S. Giovanni Gerosolimitano

Child and Saint Secondiano and Caterina (Angelo Campanella 1796), the Crucifixion with the Virgin, S. Giovanni e S.Crispino e S.Crispiniano (Bartolomeo Cavarozzi, first quarter of the XVII century) and S. Sebastiano (Francesco Romanelli, 1650).

The church, small and not very ornamented, has only one nave. The holy image on the back side gave the name to the temple. It is called church of Presentazione (the Presentation).

As recorder by a gravestone, here were temporally buried Letizia Ramolino (died in 1836), and Napoleone Bonaparte's mother, the uncle of the Emperor, Joseph Fesch, the archbishop of Lione, cardinal and grand almoner of the Empire living in Rome from 1815.

The church of S. Giovanni Gerosolimitano, built between the end of the XII and the beginning of the XIII century, was owned by the Knights of Malta, who had been present in Corneto for several centuries.

The prestigious temple was an inducement to people of Corneto to bury their dead in it.

Subject to fire, the church of S. Giovanni was repaired in various parts. The present barrel vault, which hides the original structure, was realised in 1872.

Further intervention, carried out in 1965, tried to give to the inside part a closer look to the initial one. The facade still maintains the Roman style, next to some Gothic elements, highlighted by the lanced arches situated in the three entrances.

Divided in three similar naves, composed of three spans, the inside plan of the church is unique for Corneto, being influenced by the first French Gothic.

Some wall paintings, dating back to the XV and XVI centuries are very interesting, even if in bad condition.

Close to Porta Romana (or Porta Maddalena), provided with a double shutter closure, mortised in the Medieval walls, there is a tower, called of "Dante" because of a tombstone, placed there on the occasion of the VI centenary of the death of the author of "Divina Commedia". In fact in the part called Inferno, the author Dante Alighieri remembers the city of Corneto. The tower defends the first line of the walls, divided by a long moat, in which are located Roman ruins.

These are verses from Dante:

Non han sì aspri sterpi né sì folti
quelle fiere selvagge, che in odio hanno
tra Cecina e Corneto i luoghi colti.[2]

GRAVISCA

The Etruscan Tarquinia had more than one port. The main one was, with no doubt, the one that several centuries later, took the name of Porto Clementino, from Pope Clemente XIII (1693-1769) who provided repairing and widening works for it. In the same area, as attested from some remaings, from 600 B.C. there was a largle Greek sanctuary, where foreign merchants and artisans could worship their gods. Around 580 B.C. there was a small sacellum, in a squared plain, devoted to Astarde, a Fenician goddess, called by the Etruscans *Turan* (the lady) corresponding to the Roman goddess Venus.

Between 520 and 480 B.C. to the initial sacellum was added a bigger building that probably was the seat of the cult of Astarde (identified also as Aphrodite, to be extended further on to Era and Demeter) and of holy prostitution.

A huge quantity of votive gifts, a big number of Greek inscriptions (most of them in Ionic dialect) and a marmoreal cippus of a anchor of Apollo of Aegina gave full information about trade exchanges between Tarquinia and the Greek world and of the similarities in the cult of both the Mediterranean cultures.

With the end of the V century and the whole IV century B.C. the sanctuary of Gravisca lose importance and was used only by the Etruscans. Then it slowly declined.

Finally, in 281 B.C., the Romans conquered Tarquinia and in Gravisca, in 181 B.C. they established a maritime colony that was slowly abandoned because of the insalubrious and pestilential air.

In 408 A.C. Gravisca was almost totally destroyed by the Goths. Excavations executed in the old roman urban area, established that Gravisca had a regular plan, facing the cardinal points, with prestigious buildings like a big *domus* provided with private thermal baths of hot water.

INDEX

Iconographic references:
EPT Viterbo
Emilio Valerioti
Fabio Andreani
Arpad
Regione Lazio Assessorato alla Cultura

1) A cemetery situated on a high windy hill is verdant: Christian oasi of the Etruscan Tartars. There is the beautiful lady of Velcha, who is still alive in the Tomb of Orcus.

2) These wild beasts, which hate places between Cecina and Corneto, do not have similar thick not even similar harsh.